# Couples Self Help Therapy Book about Relationships that Need Work

## Improve Communication, Love, Fun & Self Worth for Couples Both Married or Unmarried

### By Brian Mahoney

# Table of Contents

**Introduction**

**Chapter 1 Why Relationships Go Wrong**

**Chapter 2 Communication Basics: How to Listen & Speaking Authentically**

**Chapter 3 Restoring Emotional Intimacy**

**Chapter 4 Self-Worth Essential for a Healthy Relationship**

**Chapter 5 Handling Conflict in a Healthy Way**

**Chapter 6 Rekindle Romance and Fun**

**Chapter 7 Steps to Healing with Forgiveness and Self-Respect**

**Chapter 8 Dealing with External Stress Together**

**Chapter 9 Setting Shared Goals and Vision**

**Chapter 10 How to Maintain Progress & Grow Together**

**Conclusion**

**Resources**

# Disclaimer

This book is designed to provide information, guidance, and tools for couples considering forgiveness as part of their relationship journey. It is not intended to replace professional counseling, therapy, or medical advice. The authors and publishers are not licensed therapists, counselors, or medical professionals, and the strategies outlined here are based on general research and insights rather than individual diagnosis or treatment.

The advice, exercises, and suggestions presented in this book should be used at the reader's discretion and are meant to support, not replace, professional guidance. Readers are encouraged to consult a licensed mental health professional or counselor if they are experiencing significant distress, trauma, or complex relationship challenges.

The authors and publishers assume no responsibility or liability for any loss or damage experienced by readers as a result of applying the information contained within this book. Readers are responsible for making decisions that are appropriate for their personal circumstances and relationship needs.

# Introduction

Relationships. They are the nucleus of our lives. They are where we experience joy and comfort and challenges, at times. No matter if you are decades in — or recently committed — or in the dating maze of highs and lows, you probably know that relationships are never simple. This book aims to assist you in restoring, regaining and **revitalizing** your relationship with a series of practical tools and insights to fortify your connection at all costs.

There will be moments when everything is somewhat off, and couples go through these stages. With all of the ways life can get in the way — work, family obligations, financial burdens, and personal hurdles — the layers of stress that complicate your partnership can be numerous. You may be bickering with each other a lot, feeling disconnected or questioning where the magic went. You may be feeling stuck, as well as confused on how you should move forward. These struggles which can manifest at all levels of intimacy do not have to be the end of relationship, but possibly just a sign, that there is a need for tuneup rather than a need for an entire overhaul.

This book is intended to be a guide and companion for couples who are dissatisfied with their relationship but who are still relatively happy together. It is not a save what is broken beyond repair mission. It is to find the love, joy, and respect for each other that attracted you both in the first place.

It is for married and unmarried couples who wish to improve their communication, re-establish emotional intimacy and strengthen their foundation together.

In these pages, each chapter features exercises, practical tips, and a contemplation or two on a different aspect of relationships: communication, self-esteem, emotional closeness, conflict, and more. Chapters are designed to address specific components of your relationship, like listening or communication, to help bring back the love and joy. We are also going to look at self worth because a healthy relationship starts with two people feeling worthy of respect and free from shame.

Like everything else in life, relationships require nurturing, maintenance, love, patience, and an openness to evolve. By following the advice of this book, you'll be able to discover the secrets of flourishing partnerships, and how to overcome challenging times, all while turning up the intimacy, even when life seems to have buried it under life's many challenges.

Whether you showed up here after an argument between the two of you, a realization that you feel disconnected from one another, or simply a hope for a better future together, you are already moving in the direction of a better future together. With the proper mindset, and the willingness to give new ideas a chance, you and your partner can go from exasperation and disappointment to a stronger love, better connection, and relationship fulfillment.

Let's start a new journey, for a healthier, happier, and a more resilient relationship.

# Chapter 1
# Why
# Relationships
# Go Wrong

It's time to Learn more about the common pitfalls that couples face. Challenges to relationships from miscommunication, unmet expectations, and stressors in different areas of life.

There are many reasons why relationships run into problems and gaining an understanding of the reasons can often be the first step in resolving them. Let us take a look at some of the most relevant causes of relationship problems:

## Miscommunication:

Misinterpretations often stem from ineffective communication, which includes expressing emotions unclearly, making assumptions, or not listening carefully. This fosters resentment and frustration, causing the same fights over and over and no solutions.

## Unmet Expectations

Expectations not met can wreak chaos on a relationship along with doubt. We bring preconceived notions into relationships based on our previous experiences, how our parents acted in their lives, or how couples are portrayed on television. Unmet expectations around financial & intimacy roles.

**Here are other issues between partners that lead to disappointment and resentment when partners are not talking:**

**Personal Stressors**: Personal stress due to work, family, health problems, and financial issues can affect a relationship. When stressed out, people tend to be impatient, angry and have no strength left for their partner, which creates friction and misunderstanding.

**Dissimilar expression of emotions:** Everyone has their own ways of communicating their feelings, wants, and complaints. A couple who communicates directly and one partner avoids discord or communicates indirectly can lead to misunderstandings or feelings of dismissal.

**Absence of Emotional Intimacy:** Working on emotional intimacy is the key to any strong relationship, however, due to the everyday challenges, schedules and anxiety, sometimes both partners put little time and effort into building this intimacy. It is important to keep sharing and expressing thoughts, emotions, and what we face, or one partner may find themselves feeling alone, deserted.

**Differing Values and Goals:** As people, we have goals and values that change, and when partners grow apart without communicating, it can lead to disconnection. Disagreements about life choices, career ambitions, or family priorities can cause strain if not addressed early.

**Insecurity & Low Self-Esteem:** Uncertainty about your partner leaving or leaving you for someone 'better' along with personal insecurities / self-doubt can trigger jealousy and/or possessiveness. And these unmet insecurities can lead to reliance or toxic behaviors and beliefs, both of which can add so much pressure to the partnership.

**Neglect of Spending Quality Time Together:** In long-term relationships especially, partners tend to get comfortable, thinking the relationship does not require the same level of attention it did before. Increasing lack of connection and affection can wear away and break the foundation of the relationship.

Unresolved issues or trauma from the past can influence the ability to be open and vulnerable in any relationship. If you don't deal with these things from the past, then the past hurt can be dictating what happens in the present and thus having the history repeat itself with the old pattern of behavior of fighting or withdrawing.

**Outside Influence:** Expectations of family, friends or society can be stressful for the relationship. Couples may feel pressured to conform to certain roles or milestones (like marriage or children) that don't align with their personal desires, creating unnecessary tension.

**Not making an investment in happiness:** With these investments couples can connect through shared interests while creating good memories which are a tool to reinforce the couple's relationship.

Understanding and addressing these challenges requires open communication, patience, and a willingness to grow together. Relationships need regular attention, reflection, and care to thrive, especially when facing difficult times.

**Consider the notion that a relationship has seasons -- and how periods of difficulty can be natural but manageable.**

Nature is cyclical, as are the seasons of relationships — separate seasons with inherent challenges and rewards. These phases highlight the passages of abundance, security, transformation, and even adversity that all couples face in the course of a relationship. For couples that are trying to navigate the high highs with the low lows, grasping this concept can be a powerful tool.

**The Seasons of a Relationship**

**Spring:** The infancy stage, the stage of discovery, of excitement, of connection. It is a period of development and bonding between partners. Spring is filled with new experiences and the freshness of discovery.

**Summer:** Warmth and security, the relationship is stable and pleasant. There is a greater degree of trust, more communication, and partners are usually more in tune with each other. Couples relish the comfort and security of mutual understanding and appreciation at this time.

**Fall:** Autumn, the time of year when change needs to be embraced. At this stage some challenges might begin to appear when couples face dissimilarities, personal development or change of focus. While fall can bring unexpected shocks, it can also help partners realign and recommit.

**Winter:** A challenging season in which the conflict can seem more palpable, and the connection might feel strained. The winter can be lonely or difficult as couples encounter challenges to test their patience and perseverance. Still, this stage can also nurture strength and provide an opportunity for reflection, recovery and development.

### Embracing the Seasons

Every relationship experiences challenging periods or "winters". As uncomfortable as these times may be though, it doesn't automatically mean there is anything wrong with the relationship itself. They signal a period during which the couple may need to re-adjust, communicate more deeply and strive for development, and find other ways of supporting each other. With the understanding that difficult seasons do not last forever, couples can navigate these times with kindness and grace.

**Ways to Manage Challenging Seasons**

**Communication:** Honest, open dialogue is critical. By being open about feelings and actively listening, misunderstandings can be avoided, and fosters empathy instead of anger.

**Be adaptable:** With the seasons comes change in people. The relationship can be strengthened by giving each other space to grow as individuals.

**Commitment:** Winters test commitment, and getting through these seasons together can create trust and resilience that deeply supports the relationship.

**Ask for Help:** It is normal to need support during the hard seasons, whether that is family, friends or professionals.

Identify seasons as they come and realize they are a natural part of the relationship process. Move through the experience together creating connections and building confidence to withstand even the coldest winter. It brings hope when we understand inevitably there will be a spring.

Challenges don't come to stay, they come to past.

# Chapter 2
# Communication Basics How to Listen & Speaking authentically

Let's explore the fundamentals of healthy couples communication which are active listening, empathy, constructive dialogue

These fundamental principles can aid in building a connection and communicating with understanding. It can help each partner progress towards the steps that lay the foundation to a healthy relationship. Let's take a deeper look into the vital skills of active listening, empathy and productive discussion:

## Active Listening

Concentrated Attention: You pay attention when your partner speaks without distractions, or interruptions. This makes them feel as though what they are saying matters to you. That means putting away devices, making eye contact, engaging in conversation based on what **they** are saying.

**Reflective Listening:** Reflect back to your partner what they said. Saying things like "What I hear you saying is…" or "It seems to me that…" can signal that you are listening and that you understand their side.

### Don't Interrupt:

Do not interrupt even when you think you should. Giving your partner time to finish gives them the respect of hearing their voice and can actually help them untangle difficult feelings and ideas.

### Empathy

### Try being in the other Person's Shoes:

Empathy means putting yourself in your partner's shoes. Try not to make it all about you. It takes an emotional effort to put yourself in their shoes and to confirm their feelings.

### Providing Emotional Support:

Give words or actions that help express and validate their feelings. Phrases such as "I can understand why you would feel that way" or "That seems hard" demonstrate not just that you're listening but that you are matching their experience.

### No Judging:

Try not to draw quick conclusions or give **unsolicited** advice. Empathy is about not being judgmental, providing your partner with a space where they feel safe enough to express themselves.

## Constructive Dialogue

Using "I" Statements: help to not come off as blaming the other party, describe your feelings with "I" statements. So, rather than saying, "You never listen to me," replace it with, "I feel unheard when.." It also helps reduce defensive reactions.

A solution-based approach is what you are aiming for. Instead of blaming each other every time a conflict arises. Try to discover a middle ground or a solution that honors the desires of both partners.

## Staying Calm and Courteous

You may disagree with the other party; however, keep the tone calm, and avoid incendiary words or name-calling. This establishes a foundation of respect for open and honest communication.

## Practicing These Skills Daily

It takes time to develop these communication habits, but with consistency in active listening, empathy, and constructive dialogue, you create a more resilient relationship. By being kind and considerate, you can establish trust that makes it easier to foster healthy, transparent, and satisfying exchanges.

## Exercises to improve listening skills:

### Listening by Mirroring

**Instructions:** One partner shares a thought, feeling, or experience while the other listens without interrupting. The listener then "mirrors" by repeating what they heard in their own words
.
**Intention:** To verify comprehension, encourage empathy, and strengthen active listening.

### Speaker-Listener Technique

You have to take turns to talk and to listen. The way it goes is that one person talks for an allotted period of time (e.g. two minutes) while the other listens, without responding. This happens when the listener paraphrases back to the speaker what they heard once the speaker is done talking.

**Intention:** By limiting yourself to listening and not replying immediately, partners experience fewer defensive reaction responses and better focus on **each other's** words.

**Empathy Practice**

The listener names one feeling the speaker may have experienced and validates it ("I can see why you might have felt that way.")

**Intention:** to seek to understand before responding or passing judgment.

**Question and Clarify Game**

For each of the next two rounds, one partner shares a little thought or experience (doesn't have to be huge), and the other partner responds only by asking clarifying questions, rather than making statements. The goal of each question should be for clarification and understanding — not criticism.

**Objective:** Enables the listener to go deeper into understanding and not into conclusions and reactions.

## Avoiding Defensive Communication: Some strategies

### Pause During Disagreements

How to Use: If a discussion is starting to intensify, suggest a brief (5-10 minute) timeout to allow everyone to cool off. Use this time to pause and take a deep breath and consider a productive course of action.

Why it works: It prevents the instinctive emotional outbursts that lead to defensiveness.

### Learn to Self Sooth

What to Do: When you feel defensive, think of a calming technique. It could be deep breathing or counting to ten, or telling yourself that the partner isn't trying to hurt you, he/she is trying to communicate.

Effect: Calming oneself can prevent us from making the default fight or flight responses but rather work through a disagreement.

## Agree on a Safe Word

How to Do It: Establish a designated word (or phrase like "we should take a break" for either partner to invoke when they observe themselves becoming defensive or if they require a moment. Both partners pause and reassess when the safe word or phrase occurs.

Effect: Prevents escalation by providing an immediate way to stop potentially defensive exchanges and regroup calmly.

With the consistent implementation of these skills, couples can learn how to listen more deeply, speak more empathically, and be less defensive, all of which will contribute to a stronger, healthier relationship.

# Chapter 3
# Restoring Emotional Intimacy

# The importance of a emotional connection

Emotional bonding is the crux of a healthy and long-lasting relationship. It goes beyond physical attraction or similar interests. It binds couples to each other in a significant manner.

Without a firm emotional connection built from a relationship foundation, most other connections can feel more transactional and shallow. This makes the relationship less likely to stand the test of time.

## The bedrock of trust and security

With emotional connections, partners feel safe and secure, to function with one another. This security creates trust, which is essential for openness, honesty and vulnerability. Knowing a partner will be there emotionally, means each person can be themselves without fear of being judged or rejected.

## Enhances Communication

You can only talk openly with an emotional connection that fosters trust. It gives people an opportunity to express their deepest thoughts, aspirations, fears and makes them feel understood and valued by their partner.

Partners at the emotional level do not just listen to each other; they pay attention and care, and this leads to respect and appreciation for each other helping to grow stronger!

## Urges Strength During Hardship

All relationships have their challenges, but those with a deep emotional connection are more resistant to the storms which may arise in a relationship. When things that could damage the relationship happen – loss, stress, money or personal issues – connected couples with an emotional bond feel like they can support each other, that they are united, that they are in this together.

## Enhances Closeness and Satisfaction

Intimacy is that spark that can keep the flame of the relationship burning and it comes from emotional connections. It bridges the gap between physical and emotional closeness, making intimate moments more meaningful. When partners feel emotionally close, they're more likely to experience deep satisfaction and joy from the relationship, reinforcing their commitment to one another.

## Fosters Growth and Self-Worth

An emotional bond that is healthy enables both partners to feel appreciated and cherished, which is essential to developing self worth into more than just a concept. When individual validation of emotions is present, people have the motivation to pursue what they want and be the best person they can be for themselves and the relationship.

Taking small steps like continuous expressions of gratitude, practicing empathy, and spending quality time together helps to build emotional connections. When cultivated, it becomes a solid foundation upon which lasting relationships are built, allowing love to deepen and endure over time.

## Tools for Couples to reconnect emotionally and ignite Emotional Intimacy.

Rekindling emotional intimacy in a relationship is an ongoing process that requires a little effort on both sides, as well as endless open communication. The Following are some tools and techniques couples can use to emotionally reconnect:

## Daily Check-Ins

Schedule Regular Check-Ins: Find a time during the day that works for both of you to reconnect. This can be during dinner, before bed or any quiet time that works for both partners.

## Implement Structure:

You may choose to structure your check-ins beginning with:

How was your day? Tell of some highlights and of some challenges.

What made you feel loved or respected today? (Recognize positive moments)

Is there anything I can do to make you feel better? (Address any support requested)

What can we do to make tomorrow better? (Plan for improvements)

## Expressing Appreciation

Gratitude Journals: Have each partner record things they can feel gratitude for in a journal about each other. You can use these to begin your daily check-in if you are short on ideas.

**Compliment Cards:** Write specific compliments and appreciations on a stack of cards. Well, nurtured good vibes — take a turns drawing a card and read it to your partner.

**Daily affirmation:** Say something every day you like about your partner — something they did, or a quality you appreciate in them.

### Emotional Sharing

A feelings wheel organizes 72 feelings into a pie chart of sorts and buckets them into these 6 groups: sad, mad, scared, joyful, powerful, and peaceful. The wheel can be useful in identifying the specific feelings and emotions you are experiencing at any given moment so that they can be addressed and resolved.

Utilize a feelings wheel — This tip may be helpful in expressing your emotions. Use the wheel to identify thoughts and feelings. Doing this together could add a great deal of understanding to the relationship.

Vulnerability Exercises — Do exercises that tap into vulnerability like sharing fear, or anything about the past, like a childhood dream.

**Quality Time Together**

Schedule Date Nights: Set time aside to have fun and connect outside of day-to-day responsibilities. Share something new to generate excitement.

**Digital Detox:** Set aside time each week to unplug from devices and spend focused time together without distractions. A walk in the park, a dinner in quiet restaurant.

**Physical Affection**

**Simple touch rituals:** Hold hands when walking or sitting together. Give each other a quick hug when one of you comes home or leaves the house. Cuddle, or just sit next each other and touch. Do so in ways that reinforce connection.

**Massage Exchange:** Set aside time for one another to give massages, emphasizing relaxation and intimacy.

**Vision Building**

Future Planning: Talk about and plan for the future. Just you and your partner alone (it could be anything like travel plans, financial goals, family goals) A shared vision helps unite and connect.

## Surprise Acts of Kindness

Surprise Your Partner — Leave a little note, make a favorite dish, do the dishes or laundry — a little sign that says I am thinking about you, will go a long way.

Integrating these strategies into everyday life can help deepen emotional intimacy for couples and foster a more nourishing relationship. Regularly revisiting these practices and adapting them to fit your evolving relationship can lead to sustained connection and growth in emotional intimacy.

# Chapter 4
# Self-Worth
# Essential for a
# Healthy
# Relationship

**Nurturing not only your partner's self-worth, but also your own, as a couple.**

Mutual self-value is a pathway to the health of a relationship. The partnership works when both partners know their worth, and bring confidence, balance, and emotional maturity to the relationship. This foundation offers couples the ability to talk, share what they need, and support each other without passing judgment or holding resentment.

Recognizing and nurturing personal self-worth fosters personal growth, which can lead to significant benefits for the relationship. Here are some key ways individual self-worth and personal growth impact couples:

**Improved Communication:** When a high level of self-esteem is present, people are more inclined to communicate openly and effectively. This open dialogue helps to resolve conflicts faster and also build the emotional intimacy.

**The Importance of Respect:** When you respect yourself, it's easier to respect your partner, and for your partner to respect you. When each person recognizes their own worth, they are better equipped to respect and appreciate their partner's individuality, fostering a healthy, balanced relationship.

**Overcoming Adversity:** Having Self-Worth gives people the ability to deal with challenges they face by having a better mindset. When things get tough, partners with a high sense of self can face whatever comes their way as a unit, instead of in a state of panic. This makes it a lot easier to work through their problems.

**Greater Empathy:** As individuals grow and learn more about themselves, they often develop a deeper understanding of others' experiences. This sense of empathy deepens the bond between partners emotionally and helps in getting through rocky phases of life.

**Supporting Interests Outside the Relationship:** High self-esteem can act as a stimulus for pursuing interest and passions outside of the relationship. This helps, to not only enhance their own lives, but also bring something new to the table. Helping to keep the relationship fresh and interesting.

**Building an Atmosphere for Growth:** If both partners work to develop their own sense of self worth and their own development, they are providing a fertile ground for one another to grow. It becomes a partnership where both individuals can flourish. Such energy can strengthen the relationship as both parties feel appreciated and inspired to do well.

## Practices in Self-Reflection and Self-Compassion

### Daily Gratitude Journaling

**Idea:** Write down three things about yourself you are grateful for every day. This may include what you do best, what you have achieved, or any trait that you genuinely like about the yourself.

**Purpose:** This activity encourages you to acknowledge your contribution and transition from seeking validation externally to valuing yourself first.

### Self-Compassion Break

When you feel a sense of inadequacy and are seeking validation, just stop and take a self-compassion break. Recognize your emotions, tell yourself that it is normal to feel like this and then tell yourself, what you would tell a friend feeling like this.

**Why this practice works:** This helps to provide more love and compassion to you, instead of judgment. After all, when you make mistakes remember... you don't know, what you don't know.

### Values Clarification Exercise

First write down your core values, second sort them in order of importance.

Then ask yourself how these values form your identity, and what decisions you would make with or without your partner in this mindset.

Purpose: By clarifying personal values, individuals can strengthen their sense of self and reduce reliance on a partner for validation.

### Affirmation Creation

Write down positive affirmations like "I am unique, with my talents and flaws" , "I deserve to be treated well. "I am one of a kind."  Say these affirmations to yourself every day. Or buy an Affirmations Audio Book and listen to them whenever you can.

Intention: Positive affirmations can deflect negative self-talk and therefore assist in creating a stronger self-image.

## Reflective Letter Writing

Write a letter to yourself as if you were writing to a dear friend. Express love, support, and understanding, addressing any feelings of inadequacy or dependence you may have.

The goal: This exercise encourages self-acceptance and compassion, allowing you to gracefully reframe negative thinking.

## Mindfulness Meditation

Engage in mindfulness meditation 5-10 minutes every day, concentrating on breathing awareness and observing thoughts without criticism.

Why: Mindfulness increases awareness and gives you the skills to recognize and separate from the desire for validation from an outside source.

## Self-Validation Inventory

Make a list of your accomplishments, traits, and attributes you value about yourself outside of what someone else is saying. Review this list regularly.

Why: This is a great exercise to remind you that you have worth in yourself.

**Boundary Setting Reflection**

Details — Identify facets of your relationship, where you are too reliant on your partner. Jot down exact boundaries that you can create to promote independence.

Purpose - Having healthy boundaries helps foster less codependency and more Self Reliance.

**Listening to Yourself with Compassion**

In this exercise make time to listen to your own feelings and needs as if you were listening to a friend.  What will you require to support and validate yourself?

Purpose - This practice is designed to help you discover more about yourself and feel and understand your real emotions.

**Creating a Personal Vision Board**

What is it: Take pictures, quotes, and other reminders of things that relate to your image of success, achievement, self-definition, etc. Put it somewhere where you can see it on a daily basis.

Why: A vision board helps to give you focus. It is a great way to remind yourself of what you want out of life and reinforcing independence from your partner's validation.

These exercises can help individuals cultivate a sense of self-compassion and self-reflection, giving the strength to find validation from within, rather than relying solely on your partner. By fostering self-awareness and reinforcing personal values, individuals can strengthen their emotional resilience (self-worth), become less needy and enhance their relationships.

# Chapter 5
# Handling
# Conflict
# in a Healthy
# Way

# How Couples can deal with Conflicts in a Healthy Way

Resolving conflict in constructive ways, a in-depth approach towards Constructive Conflict Resolution.

## Active Listening:

Listen without formulating your reply as your partner talks. Indicate that you are engaged (including verbal and non-verbal cues [nodding, eye-contact].

Repeat what they said back in your own words, which confirms understanding and validates emotions.

## Stay Calm:

Be calm when approaching conflict. Take a few deep breaths or go on a short break if the emotions are really high.

Be respectful and don't shout...
This will keep defensiveness to a minimum. Try to expresses your feelings, without making it seem like you are blaming your partner.

### Identify the Issue:

Identify what the real problem is. Don't raise other issues, and be precise on the cause of the conflict. Acknowledge what you are both addressing so you can keep the conversation on track.

### Collaborative Problem Solving (CPS):

Collaborate to solve problems instead of competing for the "correct" response. That will include considering options, and being flexible. Make a decision on the pros and cons of the solutions together.

### Establish Boundaries:

Establish ground rules about what can be discussed and when, including a ban on name-calling, and dredging up past grievances.

Decide how long you are going to talk about this issue and when you will come back to it if necessary.

### Recognizing Harmful Patterns

Some behaviors can be toxic for healthy communication and conflicts. The first step to tackling them is recognizing these patterns.

**Stonewalling:**

That's when one partner collapses, shuts down, or disengages from the conversation.

For instance, Providing single-word answers, ignoring eye contact, exiting the room, are all signs.

So you want to work around this challenge by getting both partners to to feel safe to express themselves.

**Criticism:**

Criticism is when you attack your partner's character instead of addressing the behavior that is causing the problem.

You never listen, you always screw things up, etc…

Combat this by speaking from your own experience, rather than broadly and accusatory.

## Defensiveness:

When a partner feels attacked, they often respond with counter-complaints or justifications: this leads to dysfunctional dialogue.

So pay attention to what happens when the conversation moves from an issue discussion to a finger-pointing exercise; beware of defensiveness. Alternatively, practice accepting responsibility (even if only partially) for the role you played in the conflict.

## Contempt:

Which is made up of scornful remarks or actions, usually accompanied by sarcasm, ridicule, or gesture.

Contempt is nasty, and in fact can lead to a collapse of relationships. Do not express any sort of contempt, instead, strive to speak civilly, even when there is not any agreement.

A couple can effectively navigate conflicts by using constructive conflict resolution techniques and being aware of the toxic patterns. Building a strong foundation of trust, respect, and open communication is essential for maintaining a healthy relationship, ultimately leading to deeper understanding and connection.

**Conflict resolution strategies to navigate disagreements without breaking trust or respect.**

When fights happen, as they inevitably do, conflict resolution is necessary not only for the health of the relationship but to the wellbeing of the two individuals involved. Here are a few strategies that assist couples in moving past arguments with the maintenance of trust and respect:

Cooperative listening — each partner should listen actively in discussions. This requires active listening, validating the speaker's emotions, and paraphrasing what they've said to show that you understand. Also, it demonstrates an appreciation for each others point of views.

### Don't Make It Personal:

To avoid getting carried away, whoever has been offended should have the courtesy to stay focused on the issue and not attack the other party. This can help reduce resentment, allowing for clearer trouble shooting.

### Empathy and Validation:

Try to validate each other when it comes to feelings. This way, both partners can feel validated and can be more accepting of each other even if they have different opinions.

### Share the Sandbox:

Rather than vying to win the argument, treat the situation like you are both on the same team. Work together to brainstorm solutions, and be willing to make compromises that satisfy the needs of both partners.

### Letting Go and Forgiveness:

Once a conflict is resolved, strive to forgive and let it go. Let Go: Holding on to old resentments can destroy trust and respect. Stay focused on the present and future.

**Seek Professional Help:**

If there is a lot of conflict or if it is especially dangerous, get assistance from a couple's therapist or counselor. They can give you the tools and techniques that are relevant to your unique relationship dynamics.

If practiced well, these techniques can help you work things out when differences arise, strengthen your relationship and allow you to continue to have trust and respect for one another.

# Chapter 6
# Rekindle Romance and Fun

Bring the fun and excitement back to reignite the spark and fire

Below are some ideas to reintroduce fun, playfulness and spontaneity into a couples life:

**Surprise Date Nights:** Take turns planning surprise dates for each other, keeping where you are going and what you are doing a mystery until the last minute. This can generate excitement and allow you to make new memories together.

**Lighthearted competition:** Have a few playful challenges or games that you do jointly — such as cooking a dinner with only a certain ingredient, or a dance battle in the living room or a game of Monopoly.

**Random Surprises:** Leave little messages or presents for each other in places you might not expect them to find them, in a lunch bag, on a car seat — to brighten their day.

**Adventure Days:** Spend a day exploring a new area or doing something out of your comfort zone together—such as hiking a new path, visiting a nearby museum or taking a workshop.

**Nostalgia Nights:** Relive your favorite dates, or things that you did together when you first met. Maybe watching an old movie or preparing a recipe from your first date together.

**Quick Escapes:** Shake up the regular course of the "day to day". If you can, organize a short-weekend trip to a local setting, just pack a suitcase and go!

**Creative things to make:** Do a fun project together, for example, paint a room, plant a garden, or build something you both like. That helps in team spirit and creativity.

**Themed Dinner Nights:** Make themed dinners where you prepare meals from different cultures or time periods and dress up accordingly.

**Pick compliments:** Make a jar with compliments or positive memories about each other. Each week, pull one from the jar and share it.

**Flirty Communication:** Playful nicknames, flirty texts throughout the day, and sweet and or romantic messages are fun things to throw in to keep things playful.

Incorporating these elements can help revive the spark in a relationship, making it more joyful and fulfilling!

**A Few More Ideas**

Date nights, small romantic gestures and fun activities to help couples fall back in love all fall under this category, so here are some ideas you may share:

Go to the movies together. See the latest blockbuster or thriller. It will give you something to talk about afterwards.

Take a Cooking Class Together and learn new culinary skills together to enjoy the fruits of your labor.

Play board games or video games that you both like. Get creative with prizes for the winner.

Collaborative Playlist: Make a playlist of songs that represent your relationship and listen to it together.

Random Treats: Pick up a favorite snack or dessert when you are getting groceries or running an errand. Just because.

### Fun Activities

**Home & Craft:** Find a home improvement project or an arts-and-craft product that you both want to work on together.

**Go to Local Events:** Look for nearby concerts, fairs, or farmers' markets and get adventurous together.

**Trivia Night:** Find a trivia night at a nearby bar or restaurant and challenge each other other couples as a team.

**The Book Club for Two:** Pick out a book that you will both read and have a conversation (bonus points if you are having coffee or dinner at home as formerly mentioned)

**Tourist In Your Own City:** Go be a Tour Guide in your own city. Check out a museum, botanic garden, or heritage site you haven't been to.

### Sharing Your Ideas

**Blog or Social Media:** Write a blog post or share on social media about your date night ideas.

**Workshops for Couples:** Look into hosting or attending workshops for improving romantic relationships.

**Creative content:** Make videos or podcasts elaborating on these ideas, including testimonials or couples interviews.

**Partner Journal:** Keep a journal together write down date ideas, experiences, and reflections.

**Go to a theme park**. Enjoy the excitement of a roller coaster, or just have fun walking around the park or enjoying the park's resorts.

Presenting these ideas in a relatable and engaging way, you can inspire each other to prioritize the relationship and foster a deeper connection.

# Chapter 7
# Steps to Healing with Forgiveness and Self-Respect

## Identify the Hurt

Step one is allowing yourself to feel the pain. Take a moment to feel the hurt (it can be sadness, anger, betrayal, whatever) caused by a particular act or actions. Take your time with this, validating your feelings is part of the healing process!! Dig deeper and identify the raw emotions underneath; Is your anger due to another emotion like feeling unappreciated, disrespected, or even abandoned?

## Acknowledge the Impact

Next, reflect on how carrying this injury has impacted your life. Notice if your mood, confidence, or even general health changes. Do you notice any patterns in the way you relate to people. Maybe you are more cautious now, or the pain you have experienced has set barriers between you and the people you love the most. By being aware of these effects, you can see why this process is worth going through.

## Develop Empathy and Perspective-Taking Skills

This step is not so much about forgiving the other person, but rather letting your grief have a little less power over you. Try separating the intent of the other person, from how their action was received by you.

People sometimes hurt each other by accident and the **moment we see this distinction,** we can become free. Think back to times in your own life where you might have inadvertently hurt someone—and see if that offers some empathy for your experience. Keep in mind that practicing empathy is a way to release yourself from the chains of resentment.

**Release Expectations**

Forgiving somebody is about liberating yourself, not waiting for them to apologize. You might find it helpful to make yourself a personal release statement which you can refer back to in times of difficulty. It could be something as uncomplicated as, "I let this pain go for my own peace."
Repeat this as often as you need.

**Experiment with Exercises for Practicing Forgiveness**

Now, let's dive into some practical tools to support you in releasing. Begin with some journaling, put on paper, how you feel about what happened and the impact it had on you. You might also need to write to the person who has hurt you. You are **NOT** required to send it – this is only for you. Write out every emotion, let it be a safe haven for all the thoughts that you have.

You may also find it beneficial to try a guided meditation or visualization. Think of the pain you carry as a burden, something very heavy. Then imagine putting down that weight and feeling your body lighten as your mind starts to clear. These easy exercises can sometimes be all it takes to change the course of your journey.

## Create a New Narrative

Whatever happened to you, you are not a victim, you are a survivor, you are stronger because of it. Start writing a new story where you are powerful. You become a person who learned, grew, and persevered, rather than a victim of pain. Now you are starting to process your pain and turn it into your power.

## Release and Move Forward

Being a forgiving person, does not mean giving someone a free pass to hurt you again. If the person who hurt you is still in your life, think about what limits you may need to establish to feel safe. It is a process, not a destination, and one step at a time is totally okay. People can only go as far as you let them. You may need to "Raise your standards."

## You can forgive even when the other person is not prepared to change

Finally, know that forgiveness is possible even if the person who hurt you hasn't changed—or doesn't want to. That does NOT mean you are excusing what they did; you just have made the decision to be at peace. Realize that they may never change, and do not be worried or afraid. Live your life and get on with values in life that are true to yourself. Every now and again that means walking away from the person who keeps hurting you. Forgiveness means you are moving on without making excuses for their behavior.

## Recognize When Forgiveness Is Not Enough

Forgiveness is a present you give yourself, but in no way should it be confused with weakness. If your partner or loved one keeps repeating the same damaging actions and starts to treat your forgiveness like a green light to keep going without consequences, your relationship might need to be reassessed.

You can forgive somebody without being obliged to keep him or her in your life. Not every person is meant to be a part of your life and sometimes, the best thing you can do is walk away or let them go, and put yourself above all else. Ending a relationship can be painful, but walking away from repeated harm shows strength and commitment to yourself.

# Chapter 8
# Dealing with External Stress Together

External pressures such as work, family, and financial stress can put a huge strain on relationships. Couples who want to have a strong and lasting relationship should watch out for some of these common challenges that can put a strain on relationships.

**Work**

**Time Constraints:** Working couples often spend long hours in the office, face demanding schedules, and travel now or then, which can keep them away for long periods and leave a partner feeling neglected.

**Stress and burnout**: Job-related stress is easily transferred to everyday life and if an individual works long hours, they might be more irritable or emotionally drained and not able to connect with a partner.

**Career Aspirations:** If one partner wants to work full-time or travel across the country to focus on their career, while the other has to raise the children, that could put a lot of stress on the relationship.

**Family**

Dealing with in-laws can be challenging. A great deal of friction or different expectations can build up tension between couples.

**Parenting Styles:** If a couple has different styles of parenting, they may come into conflict. This will eventually cause disagreement and resentment between each other.

**Extended Family Responsibilities:** Instead of nurturing one another, aging parents, or siblings can have a strain on a relationship, taking time and energy away from the couple.

**Money Woes:**

**Financial Stress:** Money struggles like debt, budgeting, or job loss can lead to tension and fighting and can create communication barriers.

**Different ideas on Spending:** When one partner likes to spend money and the other prefers to save it. This difference can lead to arguments and frustration.

**Financial Goals**: Differences over financial goals — like prioritizing saving up for a home or spending on experiences — can lead to conflict.

**Other External Factors**

**Social Life:** Friends, entertaining relatives, and other social gatherings sometimes put pressure on couples, leading to feelings of overwhelm.

**Health Issues:** Physical or mental health issues can challenge any relationship, as one partner may need to take on extra responsibilities or may have difficulty providing for the other's emotional needs.

Changes in life can also cause stress between couples. Moving, job changes or the arrival of a child, can affect the delicate balance in a relationship.

**Strategies for dealing with External Stress Challenges**

**Open Communication:** Talking about emotions, apprehensions, and desires on a frequent basis may keep both partners on the same page and assist to find similar ideas to solve problems.

**Quality Time Together:** Prioritizing your union and time together, can strengthen the bond of a couple. Even small doses of quality time can help partners reconnect.

**Financial Planning** — Building a financial plan together can help keep couples on the same page, as well as help ease any tensions associated with money.

Set Boundaries: Set time aside for family or put time limits on work to keep life balance in the relationship.

Reach out for Help: If external pressures become overwhelming, couples may benefit from therapy or counseling to address deeper issues and improve their communication skills.

By being able to recognize and address the external factors that can strain a relationship, couples can work together to create a supportive environment that nurtures their bond.

**How to support one another in stressful situations**

**Learn to Recognize Stress Triggers**

As a couple, learn to identify signs of each others stress triggers. Certain words used, irritability, withdrawal etc. Discover what caused it to manifest.

Back off in the moment, and let cooler heads prevail at a another time. Try to address it within a day or two while the event and emotions are still fresh. Discuss whether or not you need more time to process, or you when you are ready to talk.

**Building an Environment of Support**

Tips for Couples: Active Listening. One of the things that couples can do to avoid misunderstandings in their relationship is learning how to listen.
Listening fully, giving them your full attention, nodding and not interrupting.

Validation: Partners should be saying things like, "It makes sense you feel this way. Making statements like "I can understand why you feel that way". This shows respect for your partners feelings can help to validate their experiences which makes them feel safer sharing the truth with you.

There is power in a physical touch, and (a hug, holding hands). This is a easy but effective way to show comfort and love.

**Emotional Guardrails**

**Establish Personal Boundaries:** Each partner should discuss their needs for physical space, time, and emotional energy during difficult times of stress.

**Respect How These Boundaries Are To Be Honored:** It is also important to have follow-up discussions around these boundaries, as they might change with time.

**Create Safe Words:** Consider a safe word or signal that either of you can use when you want to withdraw from a conversation/situation.

**Effective Communication**

Utilize I Statements (Example - "I feel overwhelmed when..") to take ownership of their feelings without blaming the other.

**Be Direct:** Get to the point and avoid unnecessary jargon or complex language. Be crystal clear about what you desire from your partner. (e.g., "I would like for you to help me with dinner tonight" instead of "You never help out me with dinner").

Correct Timing — Try to have these conversations when things are relatively calm and not during a moment of high-stress.

Encourage feedback and be open to constructive criticism.

## Practice of empathy and compromise

Perspective Taking: "If I were You" exercises have couples switch perspectives and actively put themselves in each other shoes and talk about what it would feel like to be in the same position.

Compromise Strategies: The Gottman Island Survival Game

This game simulates a survival situation where couples must choose which items are most important to them from a list of 20. Each partner ranks their choices and then they work together to create a joint list of 10. This exercise helps couples prioritize their needs and find common ground.

## Regular Check-Ins

Set Up Talks: Build regular check-ins where partners discuss stressors, needs, and how well they feel supported.

## Resources and Tools

Books

### Nonviolent Communication: A Language of Life
by Marshall B. Rosenberg

Focuses on empathetic communication and resolving conflicts without blame or criticism. It's excellent for anyone looking to create more compassionate and understanding dialogues in relationships.

### The Seven Principles for Making Marriage Work
by John Gottman

This classic dives into research-backed principles that strengthen relationships. It covers everything from conflict resolution to building friendship and intimacy with your partner.

**Attached: The New Science of Adult Attachment and How It Can Help You Find—and Keep—Love**
by Amir Levine and Rachel Heller

Examines how attachment styles impact relationships, offering practical advice on better understanding yourself and your partner.

**Hold Me Tight: Seven Conversations for a Lifetime of Love**
by Dr. Sue Johnson

Uses emotionally focused therapy to guide couples through essential conversations to strengthen their bonds and emotional connection.

**Crucial Conversations: Tools for Talking When Stakes Are High**
by Kerry Patterson, Joseph Grenny, Ron McMillan, and Al Switzler

This book provides tools to navigate high-stakes conversations with confidence and clarity, which is helpful in both personal and professional relationships.

It might be a good idea that each partner select a book for both of you to read.

Sometimes it's not what is said, but who said it. If you both take advantage of reading the same relationship books then each partner can realize that the advice given is likely not biase because it comes from a impartial source.

When couples receive these tools and strategies, they will gain the knowledge needed to create a stronger partnership. Commit to each other with regular practice, and create a space where each partner can feel heard and valued, even when under stress.

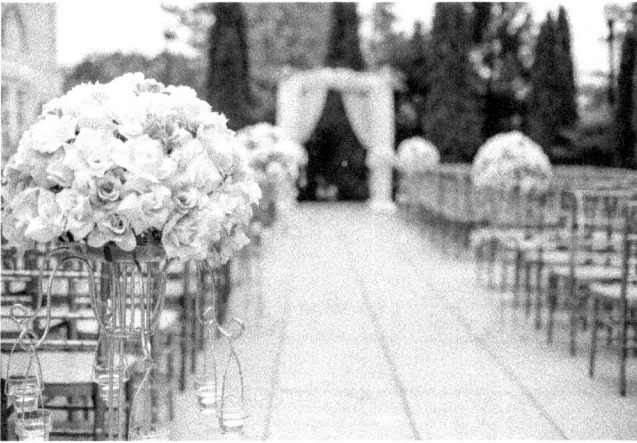

# Chapter 9
# Setting
# Shared Goals
# and Vision

This is when you are not only planning, but also strengthening a foundation of agreement, commitment and enthusiasm about what the future looks like as you establish common goals and vision. This chapter allows you to understand exactly what each one of you wants and aligns your separate idyllic dreams as well as your strengths to create a joint path forward to walk on together.

**Why Shared Goals Matter**

Consider your relationship as a journey on which you are both travelers — one in which the final destination can only be achieved together. Your relationship needs direction and purpose, shared goals help to define that destination. Without them, partners have the potential to drift apart, pursuing their own passions and dreams not realizing that they are heading in different directions. However, when you share the same goals, you're constantly moving forward as a team, facing the challenges of life with a common objective.

Having goals together will also help bring you closer. Setting goals as a couple means that you have each others back, through everything. This is a  powerful way of saying to one another, I care about us and our future.

## How Couples can Create Their Vision

Now, before you get into your individual or specific goals together, always start with a vision — an idea of what you would want your life to look like together. So take some time to dream together. Visualize yourself 20, 30 or even 50 years from now looking back on your life together as a couple. What kind of memories do you want to create? What values do you want to see upheld? Things like how you want to spend your days, and the journeys you will go on, and what you will do for others.

Ask yourselves:

How do we envision a life shared together that we both love?

As a couple, what do we value the most?

What is our vision of growth, as individuals and together?

What do we want to achieve? Build a family? Create a legacy? Or just live the best life we can full of joy. What makes meaningful life to us?

Talk through these questions, listen to each others dreams and get inspired. This vision will be your guiding light in the goals that you set.

**Goals that Reinforce Your Vision**

When you have a clear idea, put some goals in place that will help you get there. Consider these, the action steps you will pursue in order to realize your vision. A few of these goals will be large, such as purchasing a house or starting a family. Others could be on the smaller side, such as a weekly date night or dream vacation. The goal is to move forward as a couple, so strive for outcomes that incorporate both of your wants and needs.

**Here is how to define common goals effectively:**

Make Them Crystal Clear and Measurable

Vaguely stated goals promote vague results. Instead of: We want to save money, try: We want to save $5,000 over the next year for a vacation. In this way, the two of you know what you are working toward, and can easily see how well you are doing.

### Ensure They're Achievable

While it is important to push yourself, do not set an unachievable target. Consider what age you are at this point in life, what capital and time you have. Not too easy, not too hard; goals just on the edge of reach make for the sweet spot.

### Align with Your Values

Create goals that align with the values from the vision you developed. Alternatively, if giving back to the community is something that you and your partner both value, making volunteering a common goal may be more productive. If health and wellness are important to you, consider setting fitness or wellness goals that you can enjoy do together.

### Set a Timeline

Goals are Dreams with a deadline. Deadlines help to ensure that you stick to what you plan. Make short (In one years) and long term (in five or ten years) goals to help stay on track. Every couple of months or at least once per year, it is fun (and grounding) to return to these goals and re-align.

## Balancing Individual and Shared Goals

Supporting each other's individual goals is just as important as working toward shared ones. Talk to each other openly about what personal goals you're working on and find ways to encourage each other. This can help avoid the feeling of competition and instead create a sense of partnership and pride in each other's successes.

## Dealing with Differences in Goals

There will be times when your individual objectives won't entirely align. That's okay. So the trick here, is handling such differences with empathy and a free spirit that is ready to compromise. Discuss the why – understanding the motivation can make it easier to find common ground and support one another if you can articulate your vision behind your goals.

Express your passion for a goal and listen when your partner does so with curiosity and regard. Making sacrifices for each other is definitely a part of relationships. However, it needs to be balanced and mutual.

## Celebrating Milestones Together

Honor the little victories together. Achieving a destination can be exhilarating but it is traveling the path that creates connection and intimacy. Celebrate milestones together — it could be a small present, an evening out, or just each of you taking some time to think about something you have achieved together. Celebrations keep the motivation high and make the entire process rewarding. Make a small investment in happiness.

## Revisiting and Adjusting Goals

Things and situations change in life, so be prepared to make adjustments to your goals. You will have to adapt as new opportunities and challenges present themselves. Keep visiting and revising your goals. Some may no longer be relevant, some may feel more aligned with your vision now than before. Allow space and be flexible, knowing that your relationship is a breathing, evolving entity.

## Moving Forward Together

One of the most powerful things you can do as a couple, is setting shared goals. There is more to it than just achieving something. The time spent together helps to nurture the relationship and help it to thrive on mutual support, encouragement, and respect.

# Chapter 10
# How to Maintain Progress & Grow Together

Relationships are dynamic and require ongoing effort. Here are a few ideas to help you to continue to grow your relationship.

## Work on a Relationship Vision Board Together

Turn Relationship Goals + Dreams into a fun project. Cut out images, phrases, and words from inspiring magazines, or do it right on your computer by creating a collaborative vision board. Topics such as places to go, hobbies in common, or milestones in life. Goals can change so revisit it from time to time to track how you are doing and maybe refine it.

## Monthly Relationship Check-Ins

Set aside a few minutes each month to talk about your relationship. It can be an informal, pressure-free time to discuss what's going well, what we're struggling with, and how we each of us individually can improve. You should have these check-ins casually, as that shows both partners, that open communication can and should be a regular part of a healthy relationship.

## Quarterly Couples Retreat

Every few months, schedule an at-home "mini-retreat" or a reconnecting weekend trip. You could take this time to experiment together — do something meditative, create something beautiful, be tourists in a new town. This approach reinforces that growth and exploration is a collaborative venture.

## Build a Relationship Time Capsule to Open in 5, 10, 15 Years

Pen letters, snap pictures or preserve tokens that embody the present relationship, and your vision of the future. After some time — a year, or five years or so, open it, and think about how you have both grown as people and as partners but also observe if you have grown apart and how does that make you feel. This is a good reminder to both partners that relationships, like people, change over time.

## Set "Growth Challenges" for Each Other

Work together to set a quarterly personal growth challenge that indirectly benefits the relationship. Example: becoming more patience, getting better at communicating, working more on understanding other peoples point of view. Keep each other accountable, but celebrate the growth together as a couple. This helps you both become, not perfect but just better versions of yourself.

## Both of you write Relationship Growth Journal.

Write a monthly journal entry about your relationship and keep it in a shared journal. Take note of your favorite memories, the struggles you've gotten through, and what you learnt about each other. This journal will let you remember the things that brought you two together and the things that might keep the two of you growing.

## Try One New Bucket List Item Every Month

Compile a small list of some fun or adventurous things you both wanted to try. Try a different thing every month.

That can be everything from a cooking class to a new sport. Novelty keeps the interest in the relationship alive... it reminds each of you of what you both felt in the beginning of the relationship and adds to the growing list of moments that each of you can look back upon with joy.

### Establish Rituals to Give Thanks and Reflect

Set aside some time every day or every week to drop a message showing gratitude towards each other. Tell your partner, the nice things that they did that week. Above all, expressing gratitude regularly reminds you that you're both in this together, and what a blessing it can be, to be a couple.

## Increase Intimacy

### Role-Playing and Fantasy

Discuss any fantasy and explore any scenario that both partners would like to explore to spice things up a little. Another good thing about imagination is you and your spouse are no longer the same people; it's a breeze of fresh and thrilling air.

### Change the Setting

When it comes to an unforgettable evening, it's always nice to experiment with various settings, including another room or perhaps a small romantic vacation. A new setting can make things seem new and spontaneous, and taking it all in makes one feel more present and focused.

### Try a Massage

The song **Turn off the Lights by** Teddy Pendergrass features a hot oil session and and in it's entirety is a masterclass in the art of romantic love making.

Give him or her a massage using fragrant oils or lotions. Concentrate on connecting through a calming and close physical interaction. It can create trust and closeness and serve as an excellent forerunner to a more intimate night.

### Yes Day for Intimacy

Striving for one day to say "yes" to one another's proposals without getting out too much of one's comfort level. This is a fantastic opportunity to find out whether you have a new preference and make a wonderful memory!

## Dance

Take a dance class together. Learn to salsa or tango. Or just have fun at a upscale club. Dancing offers a way for couples to connect on a deeper level. The physical intimacy of holding each other close, the synchronized movements, and the shared experience of creating music together can foster a sense of unity and understanding. It can also give you a reason to dress up and feel like a million bucks!!!

## View a Romantic Movie

Have popcorn in bed, as you view romantic classics that inspire passion and being together. Casablanca, Titanic, The Notebook, Dear John, La La Land, When Harry met Sally, Serendipity, Meet Joe Black, Love and Basketball, Southside with You, Disney's live action Cinderella (2015) just to name a few.

## Play a Romantic Playlist of Music

Nothing like music to put you in the mood. John Legend's "You and I" a perfect datenight song or his "Stay with you" a song about a never ending commitment to the relationship. You can find playlists for whatever type of romantic music you like on YouTube. Or just buy a greatest hits CD of your favorite artists.

These are just a few ideas, but not the only ideas. Take the time to See what other ideas, you and your partner can come up with. To keep your relationship exciting and to grow together.

# Conclusion

Well done! You have embarked on the path to grow and strengthen your relationship. In this book, you have been given the fundamental aspects of a good relationship — communication, emotional intimacy, forgiveness, self-worth, and more. By completing these chapters, you now have the tools to nurture your relationship and your individual well-being.

Nothing worth having comes easy … relationships take constant work. And sometimes fun and excitement.

This book has been a starting point — but the actual challenge lies in the daily decisions that you and your partner make, to create your future. Making the decision to listen, the decision to forgive, the decision to choose joy in being with one another — this can be your path forward. When you remain committed to each other and you face the challenges that come your way as a couple.

Keep in mind that a relationship is a journey. There's no perfect destination, no final step after which you're done.. Each stage of life will offer its own adventures, joys, and challenges but you now have the tools to handle them with grace, respect and love.

Set check-in dates (relationship tune ups) with your partner so you can see how far you have come, and reset your goals together if necessary, to re-establish priorities, and keep the lines of communication open.

These small moments of connection can make a profound difference over time. "Inch by inch life's a cinch."

I want to thank you for the purchase of this book. May these lessons here be a resource you can refer to whenever you need, and may the love, joy, and the potential you and your partner hold together never be forgotten. With receptiveness, respect and adventure, you are poised to build a healthy relationship that will last when you both continue to thrive, create joy and lean on one another.

May you have love and happiness as you make the rest of your life, the best of your life.

# Resources: Inspirational Quotes for Self-Worth, Communication and Having Fun

This section is filled with timeless wisdom to inspire you in cultivating self-worth, deepening communication, and rediscovering the joy of having fun together. From ancient philosophers to modern voices, these quotes serve as reminders of the principles that keep a relationship healthy and vibrant.

## On Self-Worth

"To love oneself is the beginning of a lifelong romance." — Oscar Wilde

"How much more grievous are the consequences of anger than the causes of it." — Marcus Aurelius

"You, yourself, as much as anybody in the entire universe, deserve your love and affection." — Buddha

"The most powerful relationship you will ever have is the relationship with yourself." — Steve Maraboli

"Waste no more time arguing about what a good person should be. Be one." — Marcus Aurelius

"Self-care is not a luxury; it is essential." — Audre Lorde

"No one can make you feel inferior without your consent." — Eleanor Roosevelt

"Until you value yourself, you won't value your time. Until you value your time, you will not do anything with it." — M. Scott Peck

## On Communication

"Most people do not listen with the intent to understand; they listen with the intent to reply." — Stephen R. Covey

"We have two ears and one mouth so that we can listen twice as much as we speak." — Epictetus

"The single biggest problem in communication is the illusion that it has taken place." — George Bernard Shaw

"Words are but pictures of our thoughts." — John Dryden

"It is not what you say that matters, but the manner in which you say it; there lies the secret of the ages." — William Carlos Williams

"Good communication is as stimulating as black coffee, and just as hard to sleep after." — Anne Morrow Lindbergh

"Wise men speak because they have something to say; fools because they have to say something." — Plato

"Silence is one of the great arts of conversation." — Marcus Tullius Cicero

## On Having Fun and Enjoying Life Together

"Life must be lived as play." — Plato

"Do not take life too seriously. You will never get out of it alive." — Elbert Hubbard

"The most wasted of all days is one without laughter." — E. E. Cummings

"If you want happiness for an hour, take a nap. If you want happiness for a day, go fishing. If you want happiness for a year, inherit a fortune. If you want happiness for a lifetime, help someone else." — Chinese Proverb

"The art of living is more like wrestling than dancing." — Marcus Aurelius

"It is not how old you are, but how you are old." — Jules Renard

"It is a happy talent to know how to play." — Ralph Waldo Emerson

"In every job that must be done, there is an element of fun. You find the fun and—snap!—the job's a game!" — Mary Poppins (P.L. Travers)

"A day without laughter is a day wasted." — Charlie Chaplin

"Let us read, and let us dance; these two amusements will never do any harm to the world." — Voltaire

These quotes offer timeless perspectives that can help you stay grounded, speak from the heart, and remember to laugh together along the way.

They remind us that a fulfilling relationship is one that values each person, encourages open and honest dialogue, and finds joy in life's simplest moments. Return to these words whenever you need a bit of wisdom, comfort, or inspiration in your journey together.

# Glossary of Terms
## Couples
## Relationship

### Active Listening

A way of listening that's all about being fully present with your partner. You're not just hearing words—you're understanding and showing you care.

### Affectionate Gestures

Those little things, like holding hands, hugging, or giving a kiss on the cheek, that keep love alive day to day.

### Affirmations

Positive, supportive words we say to each other or ourselves, reminding ourselves and our partner of the things we love and appreciate about them.

### Appreciation Rituals

Simple daily or weekly acts that show gratitude, like saying "thank you" or recognizing something thoughtful your partner did.

### Attachment Repair

When there's been a setback in trust, attachment repair is the way couples work to rebuild that sense of security and safety.

### Attachment Style

The way we naturally connect with others, based on our earliest relationships. This can be secure, anxious, avoidant, or a mix of styles.

### Boundaries

Personal limits we set to keep ourselves and our relationship healthy—essentially, knowing what's okay and what isn't.

### Codependency

A dynamic where one person might rely heavily on the other for emotional support, sometimes at the cost of their own needs or independence.

### Collaborative Problem Solving

Tackling issues as a team! Working together to find solutions that fit both partners' needs.

### Conflict Avoidance

When one or both partners dodge disagreements to keep the peace. This can prevent issues from being fully addressed.

## Conflict Resolution

The process of handling disagreements in a healthy way, focusing on mutual understanding instead of trying to "win."

## Contempt

Showing disrespect or treating your partner like they're beneath you. It's a major relationship red flag!

## Couple's Therapy

Guided sessions with a therapist to help couples address challenges, improve communication, and strengthen their relationship.

## Criticism

Pointing out flaws in your partner's character rather than addressing specific behaviors. It's usually unproductive and hurtful.

## Defensive Communication

A reaction where one partner feels the need to protect themselves, often by blaming the other, which can escalate tension.

### Digital Detox

Taking a break from phones, tablets, and computers to reconnect and focus on quality time together.

### Effective Communication

Expressing thoughts and feelings clearly, while also listening to your partner's side—crucial for mutual understanding.

### Emotional Intimacy

A closeness where both partners feel understood, accepted, and safe to share their true selves.

### Emotional Regulation

The ability to manage our emotions in a way that keeps things constructive, especially during disagreements.

### Empathy

Understanding and feeling what your partner is going through. It's a key ingredient for emotional connection.

## Fair Fighting

Approaching conflict with respect, avoiding insults or blaming, and focusing on finding solutions.

## Forgiveness

Letting go of anger or resentment after a hurt. It doesn't mean forgetting—it means deciding to move forward.

## Fun Dates

Special outings or activities that add playfulness back into your relationship, helping you reconnect.

## Gaslighting

A form of manipulation where one partner makes the other doubt their own thoughts or feelings.

## Growth Mindset

Believing that, with effort, both you and the relationship can grow stronger over time.

### Intimacy Rebuilding

Working to restore emotional or physical closeness after a period of disconnection.

### Love Languages

The five main ways people express love: words of affirmation, quality time, receiving gifts, acts of service, and physical touch.

### Micro-Connections

Quick moments of connection throughout the day, like a kind text or smile, to show you're thinking of each other.

### Mindfulness

Staying present and aware of what's happening in the moment, which can help couples better understand each other's emotions.

### Mindfulness Meditation

A practice for calming the mind and becoming more in tune with ourselves, helping with self-regulation and communication.

### Mirror Listening

Repeating back what your partner says, not just to show you understand, but to help them feel heard.

### Nonverbal Communication

The unspoken part of communication—body language, facial expressions, tone of voice. It often says more than words!

### Personal Finance

Handling money in a way that supports both partners' goals and values, reducing financial stress in the relationship.

### Playfulness

Adding light-hearted fun, joking around, and not taking everything too seriously. It keeps things fresh and exciting!

### Projection

Attributing your own feelings or issues to your partner, which can create misunderstandings if left unchecked.

### Reflective Letter Writing

Writing down your thoughts and feelings in a letter to get clarity before talking with your partner about sensitive issues.

### Reflective Listening

Repeating back what your partner has said to confirm understanding, building trust and clarity in conversations.

### Reconnection Rituals

Regular habits like a weekly date night that help keep the relationship close, even during busy times.

### Repair Attempts

Little efforts to make up or ease tension, like a joke, smile, or apology, when a conflict has gone off track.

### Resentment

Lingering negative feelings from past issues that haven't been resolved. It can build up and harm the relationship.

### Respectful Disagreement

When partners express differing opinions while still respecting each other's point of view.

### Romantic Gestures

Thoughtful acts like planning a surprise or writing a love note that rekindle passion and show you care.

### Safe Word

A word or phrase that either partner can use to pause a conversation or take a break during a heated moment.

### Self-Awareness

Understanding your own emotions, patterns, and triggers, which helps you engage with your partner more effectively.

### Self-Love

Taking time to nurture and value yourself. When you feel good about yourself, it's easier to be a better partner.

### Setting Boundaries

Knowing and communicating your personal limits to protect yourself and keep the relationship healthy.

### Shared Goals

Dreams or objectives you're both working toward together, building teamwork and shared purpose.

### Speaker-Listener Technique

A method for taking turns speaking and listening, helping both partners feel truly heard.

### Spontaneity

Adding unplanned moments or adventures to keep the relationship fun and unexpected.

### Stonewalling

When one partner shuts down or withdraws during a conflict. It often signals feeling overwhelmed.

## Stress Management

Finding ways to handle stress so that it doesn't spill over into the relationship.

## Teamwork

Supporting each other in challenges and making decisions together. It's all about having each other's backs.

## Triggers

Situations or words that spark a strong emotional reaction, often tied to past experiences.

## Trust

Believing in each other's reliability and honesty—it's the foundation of any healthy relationship.

## Unmet Needs

When important needs in the relationship aren't being addressed, leading to potential frustration or conflict.

### Validation

Acknowledging and accepting your partner's feelings or experiences as real and meaningful, even if you don't fully agree.

### Visioning Together

Creating a shared dream for your future, from big goals to small everyday plans, to keep you on the same page.

### Vulnerability

Being open and honest, even about your fears or insecurities, to build a deeper emotional connection.

### Withdrawal

Pulling away, either emotionally or physically, during a conflict. It often signals feeling overwhelmed or disconnected.

This appendix is designed to make key relationship concepts easy to understand and apply in your own relationship journey.

Finally, if you enjoyed this book, please take the time to share your thoughts and post a review on Amazon. It'd be greatly appreciated!

Many Thanks,

Brian Mahoney

We want to thank you for the purchase of this book and more importantly, thank you for reading it to the end.  We hope your reading experience was pleasurable and that you would inform your family and friends on (Meta) Facebook, (X) Twitter or other social media.

We would like to continue to provide you with high-quality books, and to that end, would you mind leaving us a review on Amazon.com?

Just use the link below, scroll down about 3/4 of the page and you will see images similar to the one below.

We are extremely grateful for your assistance.

Warm Regards,

**Brian Mahoney**

MahoneyProducts Publishing

Book Link:
https://www.amazon.com/dp/B0DMDD4W6L

## Customer reviews

*4.6 out of 5 stars*    4.6 out of 5
6 global ratings

| | | |
|---|---|---|
| 5 star | | 64% |
| 4 star | | 36%- |
| 3 star 0% (0%) | | 0% |
| 2 star 0% (0%) | | 0% |
| 1 star 0% (0%) | | |

Review this product
Share your thoughts with other customers
(Write a Customer Review)

You might also enjoy:

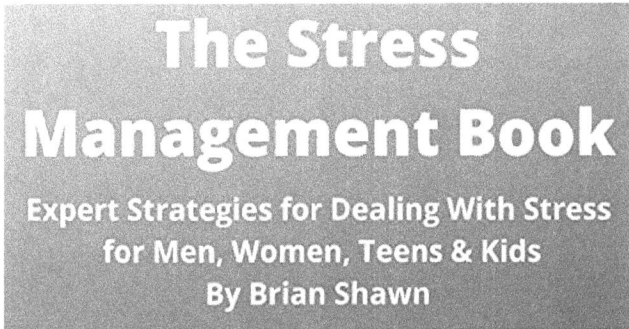

https://www.amazon.com/
dp/B09419FG8H

www.ingramcontent.com/pod-product-compliance
Lightning Source LLC
Chambersburg PA
CBHW070124030426
42335CB00016B/2257